AT LAKE SCUGOG

PRINCETON SERIES OF CONTEMPORARY POETS
Paul Muldoon, *series editor*

An Alternative to Speech, David Lehman

At Lake Scugog, Troy Jollimore

Before Recollection, Ann Lauterbach

Boleros, Jay Wright

Carnations, Anthony Carelli

The Eternal City, Kathleen Graber

The Expectations of Light, Pattiann Rogers

An Explanation of America, Robert Pinsky

For Louis Pasteur, Edgar Bowers

Hybrids of Plants and of Ghosts, Jorie Graham

In the Absence of Horses, Vicki Hearne

Operation Memory, David Lehman

Pass It On, Rachel Hadas

Reservations, James Richardson

Sadness and Happiness, Robert Pinsky

Selected Poems of Jay Wright, Jay Wright

Signs and Wonders, Carl Dennis

A Wandering Island, Karl Kirchwey

A Woman Under the Surface: Poems and Prose Poems, Alicia Ostriker

Yellow Stars and Ice, Susan Stewart

AT LAKE SCUGOG

Poems

Troy Jollimore

PRINCETON UNIVERSITY PRESS

Princeton & Oxford

for Taryn

Published by Princeton University Press, 41 William Street, Princeton,
New Jersey 08540

In the United Kingdom: Princeton University Press, 6 Oxford Street,
Woodstock, Oxfordshire OX20 1TW

press.princeton.edu

LIBRARY OF CONGRESS CATALOGING-IN-PUBLICATION DATA
Jollimore, Troy A., 1971–
   At Lake Scugog : poems / Troy Jollimore.
      p. cm. — (Princeton series of contemporary poets)
   ISBN 978-0-691-14942-4 (cloth : alk. paper)—ISBN 978-0-691-14943-1
   (pbk : alk. paper)
   I. Title.
   PR9199.4.J658A92 2011
   811'.6 — dc22   2010035408

British Library Cataloging-in-Publication Data is available

This book has been composed in Adobe Garamond

Printed on acid-free paper. ∞

Printed in the United States of America

10 9 8 7 6 5 4 3 2 1

Sometimes it hurts, boy, playing hide-and-seek inside your own head, but that's where most people find themselves most of the time, so you make the most of it.

Barry Callaghan, *Beside Still Waters*

CONTENTS

I   BURN BAG   1

The Solipsist   3
At Lake Scugog   5
Regret   7
Stain   9
Lobsters   10
Nostalgia   11
In the Lobby of the Chancellor Hotel   14
Meme, I, Self, and Eye   16
Ars Poetica   19
On Location   20
Love Poem   21
The Errand   22

II   TOM THOMSON IN FLIGHT   23

III   IMPERCEPTIBLY   41

IV   THE STARS, THE HIGHWAYS   55

Want   57
Gate   58
Free Rider   59
Two Hearts   62
Advisory   65
Organ Music   66
Workshop Poems   71
Promise   73
To His Lover   74
The Hunter   75
Remembered Summer   77
His Master's Voice   78

Acknowledgments   88

I   BURN BAG

THE SOLIPSIST

Don't be misled:
that sea-song you hear
when the shell's at your ear?
It's all in your head.

That primordial tide—
the slurp and salt-slosh
of the brain's briny wash—
is on the inside.

Truth be told, the whole place,
everything that the eye
can take in, to the sky
and beyond into space,

lives inside of your skull.
When you set your sad head
down on Procrustes' bed,
you lay down the whole

universe. You recline
on the pillow: the cosmos
grows dim. The soft ghost
in the squishy machine,

which the world is, retires.
Someday it will expire.
Then all will go silent
and dark. For the moment,

however, the black-
ness is just temporary.
The planet you carry
will shortly swing back

from the far nether regions.
And life will continue—
but only *within* you.
Which raises a question

that comes up again and again,
as to why
God would make ear and eye
to face *outward*, not in?

AT LAKE SCUGOG

1

Where what I see comes to rest,
at the edge of the lake,
against what I think I see

and, up on the bank, who I am
maintains an uneasy truce
with who I fear I am,

while in the cabin's shade, the gap between
the words I said
and those I remember saying

is just wide enough to contain
the remains that remain
of what I assumed I knew.

2

Out in the canoe, the person I thought you were
gingerly trades spots
with the person you are

and what I believe I believe
sits uncomfortably next to
what I believe.

When I promised *I will always give you
what I want you to want,*
you heard, or desired to hear,

something else. As, over and in the lake,
the cormorant and its image
traced paths through the sky.

REGRET

I'd like to take back my not saying to you
those things that, out of politeness, or caution,
I kept to myself. And, if I may—
though this might perhaps stretch the rules—I'd like
to take back *your* not saying some of the things
that you never said, like "I love you" and "Won't you
come home with me," or telling me, which
you in fact never did, perhaps in the newly
refurbished café at the Vancouver Art
Gallery as fresh drops of the downpour from which
we'd sought shelter glinted in your hair like jewels,
or windshields of cars as seen from a plane
that has just taken off or is just coming in
for a landing, when the sun is at just the right angle,
that try as you might, you could not imagine
a life without me. The passionate spark
that would have flared up in your eye as you said this—
if you had said this—I dream of it often.
I won't take those back, those dreams, though I would,
if I could, take back your not kissing me, openly,
extravagantly, not caring who saw,
or those looks of anonymous animal longing
you'd throw everyone else in the room. I'd like
to retract my retracting, just before I grabbed you,
my grabbing you on the steps of the New York
Public Library (our failure to visit
which I would also like to recall)
and shouting for all to hear, "You, you
and only you!" Yes, I'd like to take back
my not frightening the pigeons that day with my wild

protestations of uncontrolled love, my not scaring
them off into orbit, frantic and mad,
even as I now sit alone, frantic and mad,
racing to unread the book of our love
before you can finish unwriting it.

STAIN

Spreads by exceeding itself.
Spreads by letting the world waver, bend,
and fold into its dark borders.
On a map it would be a poorly-known nation
seething with imperial ambition.
Or it's something one found on the leaves of a book,
where it has blotted out the crucial word,
the puzzle-piece that reveals the murderer's
identity, the name of the girl that sent
the love letter, the ultimate fate of the star-
(or double-)crossed lovers. Or else on my skin,
like a tattoo I asked to have put there, or
the birthmark that canceled my childhood.
What land grew the plant whose powder composed
this ink? What ships carried it in what bottles?
I have seen it half-flashed, subliminally sensed
against a blank field of sky
through whose invisible perforations
the starlight would soon come flooding.
I think I have seen it coiled and concealed
like a viper deep in my lover's glance,
or spread on the crust of my heart or lung
in the spectral eye of the x-ray.
It is, perhaps, my signature,
or that of the one who released me. Or merely
an insect, squashed between the ponderous pages
of the definitive work on something or other
by some impertinent reader.

LOBSTERS

tend to cluster in prime numbers, sub-
oceanic bundles of bug consciousness
submerged in waking slumber, plunged in pits
of murk-black water. They have coalesced

out of the pitch and grime and salt suspended
within that atmospheric gloom. Their skin
is colorless below. But when exposed
to air, they start to radiate bright green,

then, soon, a siren red that wails: *I'm dead.*
The meat inside, though, is as white as teeth,
or the hard-boiled egg that comes to mind
when one cracks that crisp shell and digs beneath.

Caress the toothy claw-edge of its pincer
and you will know the single, simple thought
that populates its mind. The lobster trap is elegance
itself: one moving part: the thing that's caught.

NOSTALGIA

That theater where they show scenes from your childhood,
over and over? It's getting run-down,
the marquee grease-speckled and faded, the floors
unswept, the popcorn a little staler
each time you make your way into the dismal
interior to locate a seat near the front,
nice and close to the action, silently creeping
like a convict who's just tunneled out, or escaped
by hiding in bags of laundry, deftly dodging
the spotlight-beams of the scowling ushers . . .
The whole neighborhood has gone somewhat dodgy:
half the street is closed-out and boarded-up storefronts,
and thin half-imagined people are loitering
in clusters, rubbing their brittle hands together
and exchanging depleted platitudes. But you're used
to making your way past these shades, and through
the doors into the deteriorating lobby,
and you do it each day, even knowing that just
round the corner they've put in a new Cineplex,
state of the art and scrubbed clean of all life,
whose screens offer you your choice of two dozen
visionary dazzles straight from the soundstages
of Southern California. Sometimes you give in,
you let yourself go there, but just to be lulled
into sleep by the lustrous vicarious gleaming
of somebody else's vacuum-packed dreams
and to wake up back here, wheezing in the grimy
fish-tank atmosphere of the ancient and gasping
air conditioning system whose roar drowns out half
of the dialogue—not that it matters, really,

you've got it all memorized, every last word,
they are, after all, your words, though the actors
take certain liberties with them every so
often, even, sometimes, changing the outcome
of certain scenes (*but she didn't say that,*
we didn't go bowling—I certainly don't
recall a montage—she went back to the library
and I never saw her again . . .). Even
if, moreover (and don't ask me how
this happens, there's no explanation), the actors
seem to be altering slowly with time,
becoming, if possible, yet more absurd
in their grand optimism and foolish disabling
love for each other. So what is it, then,
that keeps you coming back? Maybe it's the knowledge
that you are the only customer, that when
this moviegoing of yours finally comes
to its inevitable end, this screen
is going to go dark and these curtains are going
to come down and these doors are going to be closed
for good. Or maybe it's the smile of the ticket
girl, the way it somehow promises
that this evening's show will be just a little better
than last night's, the pratfalls and alleged witticisms
just a bit funnier, the sickly-sweet smiles
and ungainly line readings of the child actors
just a little less grating. And who will play *her*,
you can't help but wonder, in the sequel, the movie
of the later part of your life? And who,
for that matter, will in the end play you,
on the night when you finally find her waiting for you
after the show, lingering in the lobby
ready to say *yes* to your murmured
do you want to go somewhere?, the night
when you finally get to slow-dance with her,
to put your (his?) arms around her and draw

her face in close to yours and kiss her,
like, as they say in the movies, she's never
been kissed before? All while you sit watching,
silent and still in the dark, and the air
conditioner pumps out its arctic blast, and
the faithful projector grinds doggedly away . . .

IN THE LOBBY OF THE CHANCELLOR HOTEL

In the lobby of the Chancellor Hotel
they brought to you a cup of frozen tea.

And as you sat and scratched the brittle pane
that formed the surface of that tiny pond

and watched the tourists in their coats and scarves
perambulating around Union Square,

you felt the panic of the skaters down
below, who ventured out onto the ice

in early fall, broke through, and then were caught
when the sun retreated and the pond refroze.

How long, they cried, must we yet wait for spring?
Or would have cried, had the obstinate ice

released their lips, had your hands' heat been enough
to thaw their purgatory and set them free.

But no. You held the cup. It did not warm.
And as your thoughts slowed to a crawl, you felt

the intervals between their heartbeats grow,
in parallel, longer and longer still.

Pinned like the North Star between points in time,
no longer wondering whether you should call

the waiter over and complain: *I can't
drink this,* you were content to sit and be.

The room was empty. The suspended skaters
had by now stopped desiring to be saved.

Nor did you long, even half-heartedly,
for spring.

MEME, I, SELF, AND EYE

Fifteen Self-Portraits

1

A wounded dog
that tracks the trail of its own blood
in a relentless loop.

2

A song that sings
itself, never quite in tune,
never quite recalling the words.

3

A clock whose hands
and works have fallen
into the void that trails behind.

4

A pair of glasses
that rose and blearily
put on the wrong body.

5

A blank page
flown as a flag of surrender
from an abandoned keep.

6

Loose meat wrapped around a periscope,
so that its feet
can find their way around.

7
The *me* in *name*,
or one-half of the meme
for *moi-même*. For me me me.

8
A voice
wedged into a larynx
like a hermit crab in its shell.

9
A floating funeral pyre
transporting its slow-burning flame
from shore to shore.

10
A supplicant
who shuffles along
on knees that have grown their own knees.

11
A chord
coaxed from a battered guitar
by a soldier's phantom limb.

12
An eye on stilts.
A wildly careening camera
that's broken free of its dolly.

13
An inward-facing projector
lighting a screen
that is its own audience.

14

A burn bag that has sprouted legs,
each paper-thin thought
slated for incineration.

15

An anagram
for a word that is almost my name
in a tongue that is not in my head.

ARS POETICA

When your poem looks up at you with those wide adoring eyes
it makes you want to slap her pretty face and pull her hair,
then make her strip and force her into some formal disguise.

A peek-a-boo Petrarchan teddy's standard evening wear
around here—at just fourteen lines, it's barely long enough
to cover up her *volta*—once the table's been cleared bare,

the dessert dishes licked clean and packed away. Then you get tough
with her: the interrogation light, the wooden chair,
her sobbed *I don't know anything*, her *Please, I've had enough*

(those aren't her safewords, though); your *Do I look like I care?*
You'll spill your guts in broken couplets by the time I'm done.
At parties you're sweet, loving, and polite, the perfect pair:

who'd guess at the sick fun you have when you get her alone?
She, dressed up like a whore in a sestina-corset; you,
making her crawl iambically across the floor's cold stone,

refraining as long as you can from manhandling those two
spectacular refrains of hers—a perfect rhyme indeed!
Black-hearted villain, sir, forcing a villanelle to do

such things: repeating lines entire, or ordering her to read
herself while you lean back and watch. But then, it's also true,
dominating your sweet lyric's not the only thing you need—

Sometimes perversion gets inverted: she's on top, and you
wear the handcuffs and the bag over the head. Sure, you're the poet.
Still, sometimes you like it best when she tells you what to do.

ON LOCATION

Even in the midst of my dream I found myself in a field
    of wildflowers.
Even in the midst of those flowers I stood alone, like an antenna,
    like a lighthouse in the ocean.

Even in the midst of that light I felt, deep in my chest, a scared
    animal's craving for darkness.
Even in the midst of that darkness I could hear the cicadas' song.

Even in the midst of song I remembered that I had been born in a
    bowl of silence.
Even in the midst of silence the words of my language swarmed
    around me like flies.

Even in the midst of that swarm I could hear the director
    shouting *Action!*
Even in the midst of all that action I managed to take your hand.

Even in the midst of that swarm, that song, that silence, I found the
    resolve to kiss you.
Even in the midst of that kiss I knew you and I would end up on
    the cutting room floor.

LOVE POEM

I ache for you
with all of the teeth
that fell out of my mouth
when I was a child

THE ERRAND

At my father's request I went into the city
to ask for the Senator's daughter's hand.
But she said she would not have me, nor any man.
It was, I thought, a great pity:

she was not only wealthy, but very pretty.

So I told her that I would stand
on the spot of earth where I'd been rejected
and each night she would hear my demand
until she recanted, and accepted.

For three nights I shivered as the constellations
wheeled about my head, and I repeated my offer.
Finally, on the third night, her father
put his arm around me and brought me to the kitchen.
We drank scotch. He told me she would not change her decision.
He gave me his second daughter as a consolation.

II TOM THOMSON IN FLIGHT

KENT: Give me thy hand. Who's there?
FOOL: A spirit, a spirit. He says his name's Poor Tom.

—King Lear

Prelude

Of all the things that modern man does well
there's one above all else fills him with pride:
he's learned to minimize his prison cell
and carries it with him always, on the inside.

Tom Thomson in Space

Some nights, when Tom retires, he pretty much
implodes: sucked back through nostril or an ear
into the starry void that lies behind
his sleep-blanked visage . . . Though his body crouch
corpse-still, sunk in suspended animation,
arid as freeze-dried food, his spirit finds
no rest—a cosmonaut, it treks where no man
(and even fewer *women*) have gone before:
Tom's Inner Self. Its never-ending mission:
to seek out a new life—one not to *bear*,
but *live* . . . Out of range now of Ground Control,
and hurtling straight through Ursa Major, Tom
accelerates toward the inner wall
—the universe's limit—of his skull . . .

Tom Thomson in Tumult

Regretting his regrets, ashamed of his shame,
mortified by his perpetual mortification,
Tom hangs a mendacious shingle—*away on vacation*—
and draws the shades. Having only his good name,

which no one can recall, to provide him with shelter,
he feels too naked and soft to step outside.
If he could feel proud of himself, he'd take pride in his pride—
but no such luck. His history is a welter

of failures to act when he should have acted and, worse,
failures to fail to act when he should have kept still.
He decries his constant need to decry. His curse,

which he curses with all his heart, is to hate this
cursing, hating heart of his. (Had he only the will,
he'd hate it for loving, too. But that takes *real* skill.)

Tom Thomson Indoors

The installation man didn't understand:
"You want your doorbell on the *inside*, sir?"
Well, yes—didn't he grasp it? Only fair
that prior to intruding on't, he give
the world some sort of warning. (Not that world
had shown the converse courtesy to *him* . . .)

Now stands he in his foyer, on the verge
of entering the outside—how will it be,
how changed since last time?—sounding patiently
and regular as Kant—every twelve seconds—
that calm announcing bell. Will someone come
and let him out? At some point. Understand:
all good things come to those who wait. And then,
wait just a bit more, and they go again.

Tom Thomson in Flames

It's a slow-burning fire, creeping up
the highway of his spine, which it will jump
as soon as it's built up the proper heat
to colonize his other side. He's been

on fire since he was born; the doctor slapped him
to try to put it out, but it just spat
and pitched and flared. The doctor said *he'll burn,*
but slow. The preacher said *we burn each day*

we are not right with God. Not sticks and stones,
but twigs and coals make up his frame of bones.
Sits in a pool of light—enough to read by,

barely—cast by the tiny torches that fizzle
at the stubs of his wick-fingers, his straw-dry
stuffed scarecrow toes. This kindly, kindling man.

Tom Thomson in Terror

It costs a fortune to have his fortune told.
The Fool—then Death—and next, the Six of Swords—
Madam Julia looks perturbed, but thinks she's found
a happy spin: *You're . . . traveling soon?* Oh lord,
dear Tom is *always* traveling: round and round
his small backyard, incessant, dog on a leash,
bat in an attic—even as the terror-
arium air in which he seethes and breathes
grows ever staler. "Traveling," he agrees,
laying on the counter *his* cards—credit, not Tarot,
though they too show men falling out of the sky
from lightning-licked towers, & skeletons with scythes . . .
It's no great fortune to have misfortune told.
He gathers himself. He gifts himself to the cold.

Tom Thomson in Limbo (5)

Ergo, his ego. Sadly, he and it
have been at cross-purposes for a while.
That gentle *I'll see you this evening* smile
and absent-minded but affectionate

peck on the check it would lightly bestow
on him as it was heading out the door
each morning are now, sad to say, no more:
often, these days, he doesn't even know

if it's still home, or left some time ago.
Ten a.m. rolls around. He's just getting started
drafting his list of reasons not to start

any substantial thing. *Cogito ergo
sum. I think, therefore—dearly departed—
no, wait,* beloved—*it's* I *who must depart.*

Tom Thomson in Flight

This is your captain speaking, says God's voice.
Welcome aboard. Today we will be cruising
at a great height and very, very fast.
People are sitting on Tom's left and right
in what feels like his space. *Please do ensure*
your eyes are closed, souls in the upright position,
and your regrets securely stowed. He tinkers
with his watch—how many time zones is it?—
and places hand on heart, which, sad to say,
was once flotation device, these days an anchor.
In the event of an event, a mask will drop.
If it doesn't appear to inflate, please do not worry.
Gravity will still be functioning. Please secure
your own disguise before helping others with theirs.

Tom Thomson in Disguise

His new face ain't his true face. People *love*
the new face—its fixed rictus of good will—
though when he's not around they call him "two-face"—
not to his face, however: that would kill

the *bonhomie*. Truth be told, he don't care.
People will say what they will say. Besides,
they're *right*: he knows what lurks beneath the sur-
face crust of skin—his memory's still got eyes:

it sees, when he turns to face his face in the mirror,
or shuffles through a photo album, what
abides there, slowly emerging, growing clearer—
what reveals itself—*him*self—as the fuse runs out . . .

For now, though, bites his tongue and holds his breath
'til he turns blue. Face it: he looks like death.

Tom Thomson in View

He's got so many telephones, telescopes,
microscopes, microphones, hidden in his clothes
or trained at him from behind the top-floor windows
of nearby office buildings (slyly leased

in the name of some innocuous-sounding firm—
STEVENS FINANCIAL SERVICES or what have you—)
that no mistake, no screw-up goes unscrew-
tinized: all errors are preserved on tape

for all eternity, and classified
at the morning briefing, the agents grimly chuckling
o'er coffee and danishes. It helps to lighten

a dog-dull job, this ceaseless observation
of the smallest of small existences. *Poor bastards,*
he thinks. *So then let's trade. I'll watch it. You live it.*

Tom Thomson in Lust

All he wants is for some girl to want him
to want to see her naked. And is this
too much to ask? He took his heart attack
out for a drink, and they met two headaches

bedecked in black ink at the local bar
who plumaged and preened over cocktails while
he let his hair grow long. *O sing us
a song,* the Sirens whined. He declined:

*My only song is my own, and it's yet
to be written, my dears.* So he sailed home alone,
leaving a vapor trail of smudged tears

and bread crumbs. Not even the crows would touch
that bread. Not even the most sympathetic
pillow would cradle that slumberous head.

Tom Thomson Intemperate

Wakes up with a head like a stuffed sock. *How wet
did I get last night?* something thinks in his brain,
sequelaed by a sick recollection-refrain:
O god. Who'd I blurb? Or who did I let

blurb me? Most likely he won't even know
'til the book comes out. Meanwhile, what's to do?
He's been sloshed, blurbed, and googled before—and googled
and blurbed and, desperate and shameless, inveigled

folks he'd prefer, on most days, to cross town
to avoid. *The curse of the writing class:
our book-blurb-brook burbleth eternal.* Sits down,
shakes dry his last bottle. That half-empty glass?

"It's half full," he mutters, and throws back the shot
(choking off the real question: half full of *what?*).

Tom Thomson Indifferent

It's not the past he fears—*that* he's survived.
The present, meanwhile, can be tolerated
(at least at present). And as for History
(historians, that is), he knows they've waited

decades to get their hands on him, and if
he has his way, they'll wait some decades more
while he lives out this lovely li(f)e of his.
Eventually, perhaps, they'll take the floor

to say he wasn't as good as people thought,
a one-trick pony from a one-horse town
with hoof perpetually in mouth. He shrugs:
say what you like—by then I'll be long gone—

the dead sleep well. And being overrated,
he sees at last, is badly underrated.

Tom Thomson in Reruns

"What is worth doing is worth doing twice."
Where's he heard *that* before? From his own lips.
All progress has its equal opposite price:
One small step for one man—as mankind trips—

(Where's he heard that before? From his own lips?)
and the echo bounces lightly off the moon:
One small step for one man . . . And so he trips
the circuit, and flashbulbs light up the room

as the echo bounces lightly off the moon
and he (re)packs, makes ready to (re)do
the endless circuit. Flashbulbs light up the room:
Quiet on the set. Zapruder film, take two . . .

All progress has its equal opposite price.
But what's worth doing is worth doing twice.

Tom Thomson in Tune

His radio receiver's fixed on Mars.
There, they play Pavement all the time. And Beck.
And, on state holidays, the Flaming Lips.
He thinks of when his own lips were on fire
with tunes of longing, songs of burning want . . .
(No man, then, matched the vast of his desire.)

These days he feels as voiceless and unstrung
as his sad Epiphone. Tragically Hip,
or merely tragic? Only the unsung
song will remain the same. As for the stars
on 45, he's realized what they can't:
no man's an iPod. Wears around his neck
the jewel case where the moral is inscribed:
We do not live the lives our songs describe.

III IMPERCEPTIBLY

IMPERCEPTIBLY

the milk spoils
the piano drifts for years
falling out of tune
like a disabled satellite

in a slowly decaying
orbit   abandoned
by its callous makers
who trusted it to do

the right thing, to burn up
before hitting the ground
that gorgeous flaming
penumbra   the eye

on a peacock's tail
or a literal eye
staring out of the one clear spot
of a fogged-over

mirror   the small
hesitation of
a struck match   before it
opens   a portal

to a parallel world
a dimension of flame
and you and I lounging
in the backyard

the scent of meat
on the breeze, roasting
or frying   or possibly
just being meat

how we fumble, we struggle
for words to describe
what we want   what we ask
permission to ask for

❖

waiting for the face
of the windowpane
to submit to gravity's
steady seduction

to bulge   at the bottom
so that the light
passing through   will be bent
at the exact   angle

how quiet   when we wait
how gently   we remember
how slow   saying nothing
how slow   we eat our hunger

❖

half of us thought
we were building it
the rest
that we were tearing it down

Not to answer the questions
but to dance with the questions
you said
and the letters glowed bright red

leaping off the page
as people say
impossible to ignore
From where we were standing

we could see   about
half a mile away
six or seven people
standing   on the train bridge

friends or strangers
we couldn't tell
the point was I wanted
to kiss you   in those days

I never stopped   wanting
to kiss you   even when
we kissed   I would feel myself
longing   to kiss you

❖

if you would just stop
pointing out the beauty
of all these things
and give me a moment

to think   a moment to
just take   a moment
to   and let me slip off
my silence—

sorry, I meant to say,
my shyness—
like a shelf-warped book
divesting itself

of its dust cover
(caution to the incautious
wind)   then maybe you
and I

could find out once
and for all time if these
(if you'd just give me
a moment to)

whether these little plus
and minus symbols
etched into our skin
mean   anything

✤

cherish the years
we spent wrapped in chains
cherish the marks
they left on our skin

cherish the songs
we have stored   in the gaps
between the water molecules
though when I went a-hunting

I reached after one
I could see   so that
the real bird   as always
eluded   my grasp

❖

there was nothing to be
that did not make him part
of the general hastening
toward destruction

so he decided
to remain apart
to choose to be nothing
to cling to his dear

solitude   as a barnacle
clings to rock
like those displaced creatures
in the touch tank limbo

impersonating vegetables
tasting the near air
trying   now that they are
bathed in light   to grow eyes

✥

a sun is lowered
a candle is raised
slowly to the peak
of the dome   a prayer

is uttered in
a thousand voices
repeated in
a thousand homes

a lock
is unlocked
a man
is undone

❖

I don't want to hear about
the phases of the moon
the seven perfect words
cheerleaders in the trees

or the woman from the suburbs
who gave herself to science
who unbuttoned her blouse
for the purpose of research

I don't want to watch
your goddamn movie trailer
in which the gold-haired tax attorney
weds the famous chef

only to realize then
that she has always been in love
with the silent boy who kissed her
standing on the floating bridge

or have you turn to me and say
we're two fish, you and I,
darting, drifting, spinning
in the river's haste and tug

don't want to hear about
the Phoenician alphabet
I don't want to lick my wounds
when it's yours I want to lick

❖

as I go on
this decrepit camera
captures less
and less of me

less and less
of anything
for that matter   O
but then again

it might just be
that as time goes on
there is more and more
of the world   which makes

each image a slimmer
fraction of what
there is for a lens
or an eye to see

❖

there are no words
except the words
he left us and
so few of those

a quarter inch
if that   on my shelf
hardly enough
for a life   So he painted

himself   a landscape
indigo   plains
spooky   trees
and he walked   into it

he has gone to meet
the world
within the world
so tell him   if you see him

how awful it is
to think of the other
books   the ones
he would have written

❖

yes you take your house for granted
that it will be there
when the hours trail away
as faithful as fingers

and the moon
its icy reliable light
ascending as scheduled—
a thing becomes real

a thing discovers
an importance for you
when you sink a silver hook
into its little throat

and give it the slightest of pulls.
Ever so gently
your tugging hand   coaxes it
out of the river

of sleepy being
as the rest of the world—
the tasks laid before you
like steaming dishes

at a gaudy banquet,
the diminishing series
of artifacts, each
its own tiny voice—

begins its long
patient fading into
the background noise   into
the deep oblivion

and as the things
of this world drift away
the strings that are tied
to the hooks that have caught

in the shabby and wilted
outer layers
of your skin   go taut
pulling you   through the wavering

sky   a young boy's
kite   that meanders
like a current-caught
raft   through the air

and into the nothingness
the air   melts into
ever so   slowly
ever   so gently

ever so

IV THE STARS, THE HIGHWAYS

WANT

Who's to say I'm a poet? I fear I want
too much: to live a life like a song
that's picked up by others' lips when I find it
has passed from my own. A wandering kiss
my spirit will live in. Your house, even when it
is empty, yet speaks in a faltering voice,
like waves on the lakeshore we both know. My heart
grows younger with time, its slow, serene stammer
like waves on the lakeshore. We both know my heart
is empty, yet speaks in a faltering voice:
My spirit will live in your house even when it
has passed from my own, a wandering kiss
that's picked up by others' lips when I find it
too much to live. A life like a song?
Who's to say? I'm a poet. I fear. I want.

GATE

Though everything on me had been scanned and cleared—
I had been pre-approved—still, I felt somehow impure.
A seraph with a clipboard sang, *Hurry up and wait.*
I wondered which memories they would let me keep.

I had been pre-approved. Still, I felt somehow impure,
like meat or milk gone bad. We longed for ascension.
I wondered which memories they would let me keep:
I had not thought debt had undone so many,

like meat or milk gone bad. We longed for ascension,
for grace, freshly aware of our burdensome weight.
(I had not thought debt had undone so many.)
We watched for the opening of the blessed gate,

for grace, freshly aware of our burdensome weight.
(Though everything on me had been scanned and cleared.)
We watched for the opening of the blessed gate.
A seraph with a clipboard sang, *Hurry up and wait.*

FREE RIDER

When did I first become aware of him? I remember standing before a painting—was it something by Rembrandt, *The Night Watch,* perhaps?—and turning to leave, and hearing the tiny interior voice: *wait, not yet.* It is possible that this was the first time.

"Voice," of course, being precisely the wrong word. It was a thought that I heard, unspoken. As one hears one's own, though knowing, in this case, that it was not one of mine. Why? Because I did not intend to think that? Because I did not agree with what it said? But this happens all the time, my thinking things I don't intend or don't believe. Many of my thoughts, perhaps most of them, are things that I don't think at all.

Like living for months on a small tropical island and one day coming across a set of footprints on the beach, one size larger or smaller than your own, and realizing to your surprise that you are not surprised. Those bent twigs you kept seeing, those tiny sounds in the leaves beyond the reach of the firelight—you, or at any rate some version of you, had known for some time that you weren't alone.

We are twins, conjoined not in body but in mind. Where is it that we come together? What is the hinge, the joint? The idea of loss, perhaps. Or the memory of some pain, some cruelty committed by a person we trusted.

He likes art museums. As do I. I like looking at the art, and he likes looking at the women who come to look at art. Admittedly, we sometimes get bored and trade roles.

What must it be like, never having the power to decide, always needing to plead, to file a request? I try to give him his way as much as possible; I'm not unsympathetic. (He hates me for having written that.) It could easily have been the other way around, after all. (*If only*, I can feel him thinking.)

Do other people have this—this constant companion, this parasite? (My god, he detests that word.) Why do they never talk about it? But then again, why don't I?

He doesn't like the way I use my mouth. (*Our* mouth?) The way I chew a piece of steak or taste a plum just off the tree. The way I kiss. (Besides, he always thinks I pick the wrong women.) For the most part I am able to ignore his attempts at backseat driving. What is that irritating noise? I ask myself. Oh, it's just the wind. It's just a noisy child some inconsiderate parent has brought to the restaurant where I am trying to enjoy a quiet meal.

Do I behave better, knowing that he is watching? Doubtful. Sometimes, it seems to me, I behave worse. If he is impressed by this, he has not let on.

And am I really sure that he has no control? Surely there have been things I said that were said by someone else. I'm not that cruel, or honest, as much as I'd like to be. Or as much as I say I'd like to be. If, that is, it's really me saying that.

What happens if one of us dies before the other? He would be trapped, I suppose. Paralyzed. Locked in. And I, if he died? One time he retreated for over a month, falling into silence, to make me think that he had gone for good. He intended to make me miss him. And, I must confess, I did. The freedom to do what I pleased, with no one to watch or judge—in the end, it was a little bit sickening.

I dreamed once that I was following a man, whom I intended to kill. It was night, and I had a knife in my hand. I was going to slit the man's throat; there was no doubt as to what I planned, or that I would have the will, when the moment came, to carry it out. I followed my intended victim through the long poorly lit corridors of an abandoned building, then out into a desolate street, around a corner and into an alley, where I finally caught up with him. He screamed in terror as I grabbed his arm, and turned—and my own face looked back at me. Then I woke, shot like an astronaut into the black void of my bedroom. I sat there for several minutes, breathing and letting the peak of the panic subside, and then realized. That wasn't my dream, was it? I silently asked him. Some seconds passed before he answered. *No. That one was mine.*

TWO HEARTS

It all began to make sense
when the doctors told me
I had two hearts.

One fatty and red,
as frequently pictured,
thumping its bloody,
greasy way
through the life I had chosen,
loving it, loving it all,
loving it all to death.

The other, ghastly and pale,
a ghost orchid
lurking
in the fetid barrens,
an interior field
I'd cordoned off
and walked wearily away from
some years ago.

Pining away
for the lovers not chosen,
the towns abandoned
to biography,
the apartment that I
wandered past each day
that might have been my home.

At night they wailed
and groaned to each other
like the last of their species,
divided by oceans.

Sometimes they were playful,
flirting and frisking
like puppies. But other days
found them quiet,
wary as prizefighters,
each in its corner,
nursing its private wounds.

There was the year when one
lived inside the other.
But the larger heart
had no windows. Its brother
could not see out.

When November came

and the air turned stale
they told me
they were separating.

When it finally became
intolerable
I asked the doctors
to take one out.
We'll have to abort it
to remove it, they said,
and without a thought
I answered

let it die

They let me see it after,
slumped like a jellyfish
on a tin serving dish.

But it didn't take.
In the long night
I can still feel it, now
even more a ghost,
tingling with each beat,
this phantom heart
that will not let go
of its claim on life,
its claim on *my* life.

And though it has taken
years, I have come
to terms with it,
this clock of flesh,
and if, as they tell me,
I love too much,
I have learned to love loving too much,

learned to love
the uncorrected rhythm
of two hearts beating
each in its own time

learned to love
the too much of this longing life,
the whispered *I call,*
its mate's *I hear.*

ADVISORY

Warning: this life contains substances known
to the State of California to cause cancer,
nausea, dry mouth, pregnancy,
lumbago, swamp fever, the blues, the shakes,
influenza, dizziness, drowsiness, erectile
dysfunction, unintended erectile function,
bird flu, mad cow disease, cat scratch fever,
earache, heartache, heartburn, sunburn, rope burn,
scurvy, dropsy, and irritability. Exposure
to the world may lead to confusion,
melancholic episodes, fits of doubt, moments
of bliss or despair. Life has been known
to be addictive, instilling the desire for more life,
or for other lives, or to transcend life.
The urge to laugh, or to dance, may be
irresistible and contagious.
Until you know how life will affect you, do not
attempt to operate heavy machinery.
We are not responsible for misleading appearances,
unkept promises, or squandered talents.
If plagued by desire, attempt to satisfy it,
except where unwise or immoral. Do not
exceed the recommended dosage. The
condition, that is, existence, may persist
for some decades, but in all recorded cases,
eventually clears up on its own.

ORGAN MUSIC

*There's nothing wrong with me that a completely new nervous
system wouldn't fix.*

—John Berryman

1

It's clear
I fear
the outer and the inner ear
no longer get along.
One's still enraptured by a song
that's not been aired in years,
while its mate, thinking nostalgia wrong,
is more inclined to hear
melodies of the celestial spheres,
in whose midst, it's said, the noumenal head belongs.

2

It knows,
the nose,
by any other name, a rose
would smell the very same.
It's all a crock, this language game:
some ancient stranger chose
which picture hangs in which word-frame,
and whose linguistic clothes
drape on which form. Or so one must suppose.

3

But why
asks eye
must I forever be the spy
for the relentless brain?
What we observe fills us with pain,
yet still it asks for more. Not that I
mean to complain.
I only want it to explain,
just once, exactly why
we can't let the lid drop now and again.

4

This skin
I'm in
fits like a glove. Or I fit it:
a fleshed-out mannequin.
It's supple—it can stretch a bit—
and needs to, to take in
these bones, who long, I must admit,
to ditch their wrap on some moonlit
midnight, and head out for a spin:
a naked, liberated skeleton.

5

The tongue
is hung
from the spine-ladder's topmost rung:
the clapper of a bell.
It loves—oh, hell, it *lives* to tell
how, but for it, nose could not smell;
how, when the air is young,
tongue tastes it first, and jealous lung
must wait. (Although it knows full well
without the lung, its songs would rest unsung.)

WORKSHOP POEMS

My snub-nosed drill
circles its mark like a shark
coming in for the kill.

My trusty handsaw:
a dorsal fin slicing the waves,
a multi-toothed maw.

My carpenter's level
helps me keep my shoulders square.
On each sits a devil.

My ball p-peen hammer's
tap-tap-t-tap on the t-tack's
more stutter than stammer.

When my hapless friend said
"I've bent the damn nail," he hit
the nail on the head.

I dropped a plumb line
into the abyss. Still waiting
for some sort of sign.

My measuring tape's tongue
and my own sing the same sad song:
How long? O, how long?

PROMISE

Your famous view
that each kiss restores

the life each cigarette
steals—so that you

and I break even,
your no regrets,

no qualms,
no holds barred way of living,

your democratic lust, your *prom—*
your *promise*—your *promiscuity—*

and me,

the ghost outside the door
keeping his pale lips pure.

TO HIS LOVER

It is a mortal being you hold, and soft.
Remember this. If you mistake me for
a solid and persisting thing, we both
will come to tears. Whereas, if you but grasp
the truth of what I am—then we'll still come
to tears; but there may first be time, before
this doom arrives, to get some kissing in.
Real kisses, *ma cherie*: rough, wild, and deep.
But you ask: *Where can we, if not in heaven,*
find such a kiss, 'midst all the plastic tchotchkes
and factory-fakes? Lips pressed against each other
make not a kiss if souls their distance keep . . .
Heaven can go to hell, my sweet. Let man
and woman join what God has put asunder.

THE HUNTER

Out of the frozen waterfall, the impenetrable wood,
he was enticed into existence one night
in the midst of a magic show. Tunneled like rain
through his father's hat, he resigned to forget
the choired, dimensionless world of his home,
to grasp the knife of the new in his hand
and carve his signature on the sea.

Knee-deep, he saw the advancing line
of his ancestors, almost lost his nerve
under the force of their palpable ambivalence—
but his daemon told him *stay*, and he stayed.

A weekend with a woman of beauty taught him
the meaning of loss. Afterward, in the street,
in a panhandler's robes, he lingered for hours,
memorizing the behavior of the stones.
He recognized himself as others did,
by his wounds, the scars of battle, whose tracks
spoke of past and future. If only a person
could tell them apart! But he would never again
mistake his own mouth for another's.

When he was done naming the constellations and each
of their pinpricks of light, he began again,
working backwards this time. He traded voices
with the one who controls the winds. He tracked down
the source of the river and stood in its shallows
for five days until, exhausted and beaten,
it showed him where its eyes were hidden.

At the end, rendered foreign, driven to regret
by the pulsating funnel of flies that was
his constant companion, he abandoned hope
of comfort, sold his clothes, and aspired
to generality: as if other lost wanderers,
too, might let their songs rest for a moment
and grant themselves an ephemeral refuge
under the nebula of his name.

REMEMBERED SUMMER

Always, in that season, came the point in the day
when our conversations faltered, the celestial musicians
took a break between sets, and all the little engines
we had so painstakingly gathered and constructed
lapsed into stillness for a few brief moments,
and around us—for nature will not tolerate a vacuum—
rising like a swarm of black flies from the neglected fields
and scattered pools of stagnant water there arose the sound
that filled our atmosphere like the drone of some far-off
crop duster, like a universal headache, like the decrescendo
moan of a piano that has fallen to the street
from some high apartment window and smashed like a body.
We pretended that none of us could hear it, which is what
humans do, and retreated like monks, each into his own
private interior garden, the gate
of the eye glazed over and locked shut. We knew
that it would pass (though we knew, too, that the day would come
when it would not pass), we knew that for the moment
there were comforts, crossword puzzles, board games to be played,
tea waiting to be poured into bright blue
porcelain cups, to give off small puffy
steam-exhalations like sighs of satisfaction.
These were promised to us. And the rest of what life promised,
we simply would not speak of. But we never stopped hearing it
entirely, that groan, as of a vast collapsing heart.
That distant roar, that might have been the planet's great slow turning.
That distant roar, that might have been the planet's great slow burning.

HIS MASTER'S VOICE

—for Piper

1

The stars, the highways we have left for you
use them well

We have broken our backs to build them

We have filled our pockets with mud, we have folded
our small, spent bodies into leaking coffins

We have traced the outlines of our limbs on paper
so brittle a single word, uttered with passion,

would crack and tear it, like a fragile crust
laid over a bubbling, boiling liquid

We have let our children grow tall
without teaching them the songs of the elders

The songs we ourselves used to sing
in the interminable, reverberating night

The songs we ourselves used to chant
side by side, hand in hand, as the stars gave violent

birth to stars
the songs we would sing

and sing and sing

to drive away the danger

2

You turn a knob: water flows

You throw a switch: the room is flooded with light

In every corner of this city there are people
waiting to serve you. To sell you a bagel

to tell you what goes on in foreign countries
to cut your hair, translate your letters

or say that they love you. And you will take this
for granted. You will say: *what else are these people*

going to do with the interminable chain
of hours the world has forced upon them?

You will say: *watch this coin, this unexceptional*
coin, watch closely, ah, where's it gone?

It has gone to every corner of this city
It has gone wandering like a lost child

It is in the library on a high shelf
It is in the woods, flashing, catching the fire

at the edge of the chamber the firelight makes
in the midst of the trees. This is the fire

that must never stop burning. This is the tale
we must never stop telling, by the light of these flames

3

As for the songs

how hard it is to imagine
facing the vast speechless night without them

Nonetheless, it is done

You will understand one day
or you will forget

You are more expert at forgetting
than we ever were skilled at anything

Your greatest feat was to forget the things
it took us centuries to discover

To forget that your knowledge won't save you, to forget
that knowing that your knowledge won't save you won't save you

Still, don't lose sight of the promise that lurks
in unanswered questions. Don't take them for granted

the bookstores, the bowling alleys

they will need to be maintained

4

The rain, for example: just how far up does it form,
and how long does it take to fall?

Why do some of the stars change position against
the fixed background of the others? When

the oceans shift, who suffers?
Can you really make a defibrillator

that's powered by a potato? A twelve-year-old
boy would know the answers, if

he could be distracted for a moment
from his twelve-year-old-boy concerns: geysers,

microscopes, the forbidding monuments
he will one day construct, or which unknown others

will build to his name, in his image, his shadow—
the languages he will learn and prop

in the window to catch the early light
or lay against those he will never speak

like cords of wood in a pile, like a house of cards
like reluctant lovers

5

Time shivering like sand in the palm of your hand
as, sixty miles offshore,

a drag-net is hauled from the water, writhing and seething,
a livid, roiling mass

of floppy quickened flesh-daggers. Meanwhile a woman
passing you on the sidewalk

or browsing the offerings in the cereal aisle
looks up and smiles at you

charmingly, distractedly
(and don't those cereal boxes look

like they are about to erupt in fire?)
her left hand tracing an unknowable figure

in the thickening air. From inside a passing
car, a song shuttles to crescendo

climaxing into a sudden explosion
of joyous noise, then fades from the crisis

(and doesn't the very air feel as if
it is gathering its forces, bracing itself

against tomorrow's storm?)
as life slides back from its latest culmination

and the ordinary words and dishes are brought out
again, the old comforting shopworn feelings—

a conspirator's glance, cast and denied—
tiny universes bloom in the space of a second

then pause and contract, retreating back
into the covert and minimal

original seeds, subliminal eyes
or fists snapping shut like oysters, shutting out

everything they are not, determined never
again to be revealed, to be

forced open

6

The shadow of a schoolhouse or church torn down
years ago still falls across the lawn

and cools the grass in the wake of where it stood
where you stand now, with mulched lawn

and soil-suck underfoot, and the sun
descending, the sun perpetually descending

The histories we didn't live haunt us, coax us
In another life you would have known her name

Perhaps you could have talked to her, talked her into
letting you kiss her neck, letting you take her

to a borrowed room somewhere. In another life
a shadow might have dropped itself across your twinned limbs

7

The seas, the rivers without which our parchments are blank faces:
do not be too quick to drain them

After the war, when the travelers came home,
we hoped they would fit back into our cities

like fence posts into the ground

like a bandage over a wound

We hoped to return to the earlier plan
to start the sequel as if there had been

no interruption. But too many words
had entered the language. And each had to be

compared with the original, as, when an orchestra
tunes itself, each musician compares

his instrument's pitch not with that
of his neighbor, but with the oboe; or, later,

in mid-performance, each keeps his eye,
not on the player on his left or right,

but on the conductor. We were groping
toward a new syntax, seeking a way

to live that was not also a way
of dying, seeking to temper ourselves

to emerge from the chrysalis as fresh-minted blades—
newly unsheathed, tinged with just enough evil

to cut against the grain, against the static
of the world's inexhaustible resistance

8

Some things are just hard: mailing snakes, for example
While others just sing and sing and sing

(as you pay and pay and pay . . .) Anyone
who knows a couple-three things about birds

knows that the most ingenious, delicate,
intricate machine can fall

to the ground in a second, re-categorized
by the powers that be with a sickening *thunk*

from "ethereal warbler" into "just junk,"
into "clod of earth." So why should our waiting

keep us from living? One is supposed to decline,
politely. But how to keep oneself

from dwelling on the pleasures of the surprise ending,
the unanticipated answer? From requesting

a second superfluous helping of plainsong,
from bringing a medieval siege engine to the wedding?

9

In the end, what is there but a small cloth bag
passed from one warm hand to another? A stranger

is offering it to you, holding it out
as if it were injured and needed care

Don't think about the matrix of her red hair,
her imploring gaze. Just take the hand

that your parents gave you and reach deep into
the bag, and feel them, those small, cool marbles

perfect spheres, as dense as sleep—

as if by suffering enough we had somehow
earned the permission to kiss—

No, don't ask yourself how much it cost
to track them down and bring them here

or who might be missing them, who might even now
be searching for them—

You cannot deny us as long as you are singing
As long as you are singing, you belong to all of us—

Just roll them around in your cupped hand
with your eyes clamped shut. This is the world

This is how the world

This is how the world feels
to the newborn singers, to the ones

who have not grown used to it yet

ACKNOWLEDGMENTS

Poems from this collection have appeared in *ARC*, *The Believer*, *Granta*, *Hayden's Ferry Review*, *Indiana Review*, *MARGIE*, *McSweeney's*, *The New Yorker*, *The Pinch*, *Pleiades*, *Ploughshares*, *Poetry*, and *The Walrus*. My thanks to the editors for allowing them to be reprinted.

Some of these poems were also published in a chapbook, *The Solipsist* (Cohasset, California: Bear Star Press, 2008).

"The Errand" was published as a limited-edition letterpress broadside by Occasional Works of Menlo Park, California in 2007.

"Tom Thomson in Flames" was published as a limited-edition letterpress broadside by the Quoin Collective of Chico, California in 2010.

"Tom Thomson in Limbo (5)" is a sequel of sorts to "Tom Thomson in Limbo" (1 through 4), which appeared in the title sequence of *Tom Thomson in Purgatory* (MARGIE/IntuiT House Poetry Series, 2006).

Two lines of "Imperceptibly" were stolen from Rebecca Rosenblum.

My thanks to Heather Altfeld, Hadara Bar-Nadav, Sharon Barrios, Aaron Belz, Barry Callaghan, Michael Callaghan, Jeanne Clark, Nicole Dermoudy, Robin Ekiss, Becky Foust, Julia Gordon-Bramer, Paul Muldoon, Bob Nazarene, Alexandra Payne, D. A. Powell, Donal Power, Kevin Prufer, James Richardson, Ann Rosener, Rebecca Skloot, Beth Spencer, KC Trommer, and Susan Wheeler.